Yes I Can:

A Kid's Guide to Dealing with Physical Challenges

Written by Kathleen M. Muldoon
Illustrated by R.W. Alley

ONE
CARING
PLACE

Abbey Press
St. Meinrad, IN 47577

To my amazing friends, Betty Minyard, Nancy Kroll, and Kathleen Bohr.
Thank you for making my crutches, braces, and prosthesis part of
your all-encompassing embrace.

Text © 2010 Kathleen M. Muldoon
Illustrations © 2010 Saint Meinrad Archabbey
Published by One Caring Place
Abbey Press
St. Meinrad, Indiana 47577

Library of Congress Catalog Number
2009910933

ISBN 978-0-87029-431-0

Printed in the United States of America

A Message to Parents, Teachers, and Other Caring Adults

When you parent, teach, or befriend physically challenged children, you embark on an arduous, yet rewarding, journey. These children will ultimately have to come to terms with their limitations. In large part, it is your guidance and acceptance that will shape their attitudes, hopefully leading to their realization that they have an important place in society.

We all have challenges. But those whose challenges are physical, and thus visible, carry the added burden of facing attitudinal barriers. This can be especially difficult for a child who, while trying to establish himself as a normal kid, is constantly reminded by the stares and remarks of others that he's not. It is your job to help him reach his maximum potential by focusing on what he can do rather than on what he can't do.

If you are the parent of a physically challenged child, you must balance your ordinary parenting duties while also navigating the world of special equipment, social services, and other necessities specific to your child. Learning all you can about her condition will serve you well in meeting her needs. Mainstreaming helps her or him feel part of society. But also consider joining a parents' support group and introducing your child to other kids with similar physical challenges. Such participation will help you both flourish.

Physically challenged kids need all the positive reinforcement they can get. I hope this book will help you to inspire the special children in your life to shout "Yes I can!" as they discover how to adapt to their disabilities, maximize their abilities, and carve a place for themselves in this world.

—*Kathleen M. Muldoon*

What Are Your Challenges?

You meet challenges every day. Challenges are things you have to do even though they may be hard or uncomfortable. Taking a test in school is a mental challenge. Playing sports, walking, and riding a bicycle are some physical challenges. Having body parts that don't work as they should is also a physical challenge.

Using a wheelchair or walking with crutches can make other physical challenges harder for you. But you know you can do many things. You just do them differently.

Everybody has challenges. Learning how to overcome them makes you want to shout, "Here I am, world! I can do anything."

It's All Right to Ask Questions

Sometimes, especially when you're having a not-so-good day, you might ask, "Why doesn't my body work the same as everyone else's?" The answer could be that a sickness or accident made parts of your body weak or stop working. Or maybe you were born with physical challenges. It could be that no one knows why.

The best questions to ask are, "God, can you help me learn to live with my body? Can you help me be the best I can be?" God always answers, "Yes! I made you and love you just the way you are."

What ARE They Looking At?

While you're zooming along with your walker in the mall, you notice people staring at you. You've learned from your parents that it's rude to stare. But when children and adults see something different, they wonder about it.

It's all right to feel annoyed when people stare. But try to remember that they are just curious. They want to know why you don't walk or talk or look the same way as they do.

Try looking at people who stare...and smile. Some will smile back and then go about their business. Others may stay and talk. Maybe you'll make a new friend!

YOU, A Teacher!

When you go to a new school or grade, you need to teach your teachers. They won't know how to help you unless you tell them.

Ask your teacher for time to introduce yourself. That way you can talk to your teacher and classmates at the same time. Let them know the things you can do for yourself and the things you need help with, such as carrying your books or being patient with your challenges.

Your classmates and teacher are anxious to help you. Try to think of ways to help your classmates, too ... like helping them with spelling or math.

More Helping Hands

Besides parents and teachers, adults called therapists may be part of your life. They will help you make your body work the best that it can.

Physical therapists might show you wheelchair exercises or teach you to walk up steps on your crutches. Occupational therapists show you ways to do everyday stuff. Speech therapists help you speak loud and clear!

Learning to be you is hard work. Your job is to learn and practice what therapists teach you. There will be days when you don't want to go, but the more you practice, the more things you'll be able to do.

Making Friends and Being a Friend

Sometimes when children see kids with physical challenges like yours, they feel shy or afraid. They wonder if you will be able to play and do things they like to do.

Is there someone who you think would make a good friend? Introduce yourself. Talk about some things that you like to do. Ask what he or she enjoys doing. You may find there are lots of good times you can share.

There will always be some people we like better than others. There will always be some people who like us and some who don't. That's all right! Just be the best friend you can be.

Be a Team Helper

Sometimes friends and classmates will play sports where they run or jump, like soccer and football. It's all right to feel sad when you can't join the team. But maybe you can think of ways to help the team.

Cheering for your friends is one way. Wear the team colors. Decorate your wheelchair or crutches with those colors. Wave a banner. Yell "Go team go!" Be their number one fan, whether the team wins or loses.

For some sports, you might be able to be scorekeeper. Maybe the coach can use you as an assistant. Being a team helper keeps you close to your friends.

Be a Team Player

There are some sports teams just for people with physical challenges. What sports do you like best? Basketball and bowling are two you might try.

Adults can help you find such teams in your city or town. Maybe there is a wheelchair team you can watch or join. In some cities, Little League has baseball teams for physically challenged athletes.

If you like the water, swimming might be your sport. If you prefer snow, how about skiing? If you like to go fast, wheelchair racing is just the thing. You might play sports differently than other kids, but you'll have just as much fun.

Sharing Mom and Dad

When you have physical challenges, your parents help you at home, take you to therapy appointments, and help you practice things your therapist taught you.

Your brothers and sisters might feel that Mom and Dad love you best because they spend so much time with you. They may also feel guilty that they can do things that you can't.

Let them know you understand how they feel. Do as much for yourself as you can, so your parents have more time to share. Ask your brothers and sisters to help with your therapy in exchange for your reading or playing a board game with them.

Some Days Everything Goes Wrong!

You wake up grumpy. Your new shirt gets caught in your wheels. You drop your homework in a puddle and then your crutch slips on it. You're having an awful, terrible day! It's easy to smile on good days, but bad days are definitely harder.

Two things can help you get through bad days. Laughing at yourself makes the bad things seem silly and unimportant. Sharing laughter is even better.

The other thing is to remember that God is only a prayer away. God listens to your prayers and helps in time of need. On bad days, everyone needs all the help they can get!

Discovering Your Talents

God gave each of us special gifts. That includes people with physical challenges. It's important that you discover your gifts and then make the most of them. God gave us these talents to use and share with others.

Perhaps you are a good writer or an artist. Wow, what great talents! Maybe you have a talent playing chess, which takes real brain power. Do you have the gift of teaching? That is a very special talent, one you can use to help your brothers and sisters or friends.

Using your talents will help you be all you can be.

Dream BIG

Adults often ask children, "What do you want to be when you grow up?" For kids with physical challenges, that question might seem hard to answer. It's important to know that great things will be possible for you.

Learning about others with physical challenges will help you see lots of possibilities in your future. Olympic athlete, Oscar Pistorius, runs on two high-tech artificial legs. Actress, Marlee Matlin, is deaf. Franklin Roosevelt, who used a wheelchair and wore leg braces, was President of the United States.

Your school librarian can help you find books about people who overcame physical challenges. What will you be when you grow up? Dream big!

Questions, Questions, Questions

"What's wrong with you?" "How come you walk with crutches?" "Why do you use that wheelchair?" You probably get tired of answering such questions. Here are some things you might try.

• Give short answers. "My legs are weak and crutches help me walk"; or, "My wheels get me where I'm going." Some kids just say, "This is the way God made me."

• If you don't want to answer, smile and say, "All I know is I'm feeling great today, and I hope you are too."

• Share as much as you want and then change the subject. "Hey, that's enough about me. Let's play something."

The One and Only You

Do you know what's really amazing? There are close to seven billion people in the world, yet God created each of us differently.

You have everything you need within you to become the person God intended you to be. You might have parts of your body that are weak, but you have other strengths that make up for those.

Your job is to be the one and only you. Once you've found your strengths, grow them. Greet each day knowing that with your strengths and God's help, you can do anything you want to do. Yes you can!

Kathleen M. Muldoon works around her physical challenges while teaching writing and authoring children's books. Before moving from Pennsylvania to Texas, she served terms on the board of Open Doors for the Handicapped and on an Advisory Committee to the Pennsylvania Office of Vocational Rehabilitation. She now lives in San Antonio, Texas, where she enjoys soaking up Mexican-American culture—and food!—and spoiling her cat, Prissy, and parakeet, Abraham.

R. W. Alley is the illustrator for the popular Abbey Press adult series of Elf-help books, as well as an illustrator and writer of children's books. He lives in Barrington, Rhode Island, with his wife, daughter, and son. See a wide variety of his works at: www.rwalley.com.